Facts About

Reptiles

DONNA BAILEY

RSVP
RAINTREE
STECK-VAUGHN
PUBLISHERS
The Steck-Vaughn Company
Austin, Texas

How to Use This Book

This book tells you many things about reptiles. There is a Table of Contents on the next page. It shows you what each double page of the book is about. For example, pages 14 and 15 tell you about "Large Dinosaurs."

On some of these pages you will find words that are printed in **bold** type. The bold type shows you that these words are in the glossary on pages 46 and 47. The glossary explains the meaning of some words that may be new to you.

At the very end of the book there is an index. The index tells you where to find certain words in the book. For example, you can use the index to look up words like fangs, venom, constrictors, and many other words to do with reptiles.

Library of Congress
Cataloging-in-Publication Data

Bailey, Donna.
   Reptiles/ Donna Bailey.
      p. cm. — (Facts about)
   Summary: Traces the evolution of reptiles from various prehistoric animals, including flying and sea dinosaurs. Discusses the death of dinosaurs, where reptiles live today, the variety of lizards, snakes, crocodiles, alligators, and turtles, their enemies, and their future.
   ISBN 0-8114-6627-2
   1. Reptiles—Juvenile literature.   [1. Reptiles.]
I. Title.   II. Series: Facts about (Austin, Tex.)
QL665.B325   1990
597.9—dc20   89-21756
   ISBN 0-8114-2507-X   Hardcover Library Binding
   ISBN 0-8114-6627-2   Softcover Binding

Contents

Early Days

Millions of years ago there were many different kinds of reptiles.

Our chart shows when most of these reptiles lived, and when they died out. If you look at the blue section of the chart, you can see that of all these early reptiles, only turtles, crocodiles, tuatara, lizards, and snakes are still alive today.

Most of the larger reptiles such as **dinosaurs** died out 65 million years ago.

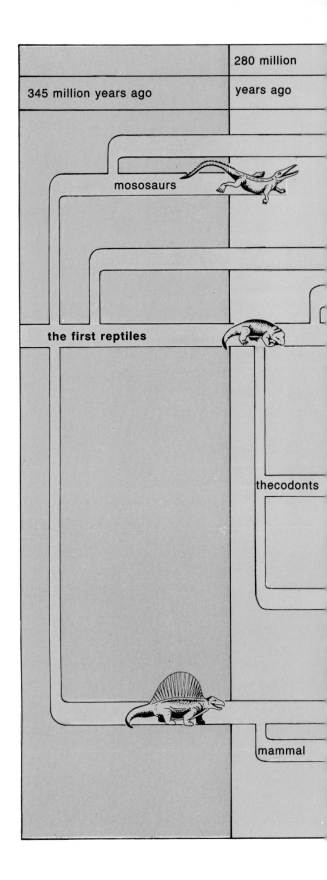

345 million years ago

280 million years ago

mososaurs

the first reptiles

thecodonts

mammal

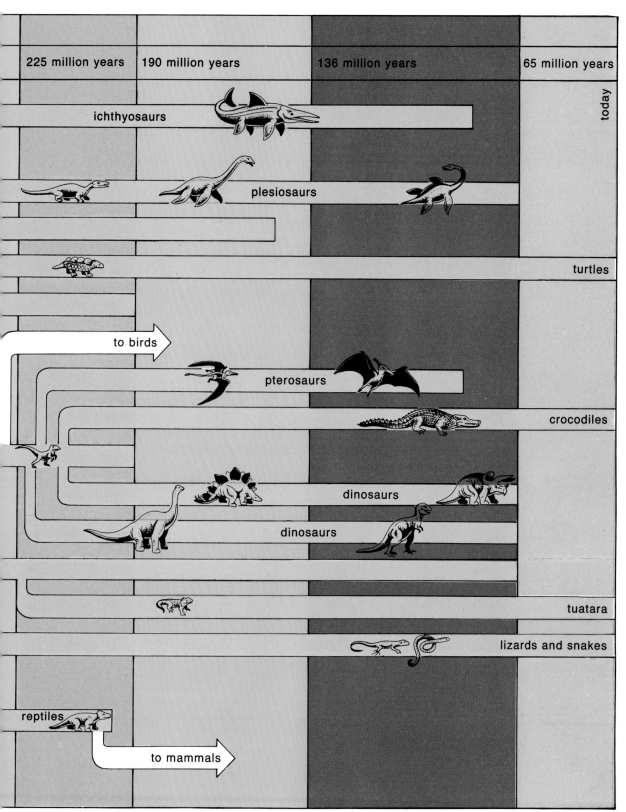

225 million years | 190 million years | 136 million years | 65 million years

today

ichthyosaurs

plesiosaurs

turtles

to birds

pterosaurs

crocodiles

dinosaurs

dinosaurs

tuatara

lizards and snakes

reptiles

to mammals

5

Before the Reptiles

Millions of years	PERIOD
Present day	AGE OF MAMMALS
65	AGE OF MAMMALS
136	AGE OF REPTILES
190	AGE OF REPTILES
225	AGE OF REPTILES
280	AGE OF AMPHIBIANS
345	AGE OF AMPHIBIANS
395	AGE OF FISH
430	AGE OF FISH
500	AGE OF SEA CREATURES
570	AGE OF SEA CREATURES
600	AGE OF SEA CREATURES

If you look at the bottom of our chart, you can see that the first animals were sea creatures. Some 430 million years ago the first fish appeared.

About 345 million years ago **amphibians** developed from these fish.

Amphibians could live both in water and on land.

Most reptiles lived from 225-65 million years ago, in the age of reptiles.

Mammals only developed about 65 million years ago.

Our picture shows how fish gradually grew legs and developed into amphibians. Some amphibians then slowly changed into reptiles.

Amphibians lived in **swamps** because they had to live near water.

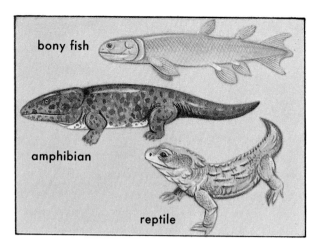

how fish changed into reptiles

some early amphibians

What Is a Reptile?

Reptiles are animals with dry, scaly skins. They have no hair. Most reptiles have short legs that stick out from either side of their bodies.

Reptiles lay eggs with soft shells.

Our picture shows a baby crocodile hatching out from its soft shell.

a lizard is a reptile

soft crocodile eggs

When a baby reptile comes out of the egg it looks like its parents.

It grows fast, and soon its scaly skin gets too tight. Underneath, it has grown a new skin. The old skin splits and the reptile crawls out of it.

Our picture shows a gecko that is crawling out of its old skin.

Learning from Fossils

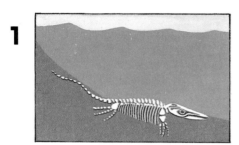

1

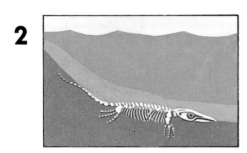

2

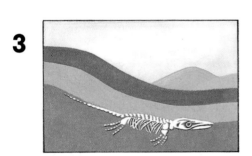

3

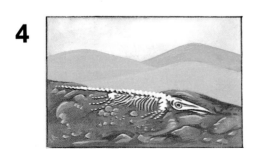

4

We can learn a lot about reptiles from their **fossils**. Our pictures show how a fossil is made.

1. Millions of years ago the **skeleton** of a dead animal sank to the bottom of a lake.

2. Layers of mud covered the bones.

3. The layers of mud turned into rock and the lake dried up.

4. Wind and rain wore away the rock over millions of years so now we can find the fossil bones on the ground.

Trace fossils are shapes
left in rocks.

Millions of years ago,
a dinosaur walked
over the mud and left this
footprint.

People collect fossil
bones and try to make
up the skeleton again.

a dinosaur footprint

collecting fossils

The First Reptiles

Seymouria

The Seymouria was half amphibian and half reptile.

The early reptile in our picture was a Dimetrodon. It was about 10 feet long.

Dimetrodon

Euparkeria

The Euparkeria in our picture
belonged to an important new group
of reptiles called **thecodonts**.
These reptiles ate the meat of
other animals.

Thecodonts had small front legs, and
back legs that were underneath
their bodies. This meant they could
run very fast. Thecodonts used their
long tails to help them balance.

Large Dinosaurs

Our picture shows a group of meat-eating dinosaurs called **theropods**.

Some were about 40 feet long, like the Tyrannosaurus in our picture. The Coelophysis and the Ornithomimus were smaller, but just as fierce.

They all had sharp teeth and claws.

Ornithomimus

Coelophysis

Tyrannosaurus

Dinosaurs called **sauropods** ate plants.
   These were huge beasts, with long
necks and tails. Brachiosaurus was
40 feet tall and 75 feet long.
Diplodocus was 100 feet long.
   They lived in swamps, and had thick
legs and small teeth.

Brachiosaurus

Diplodocus

Plant-eating Dinosaurs

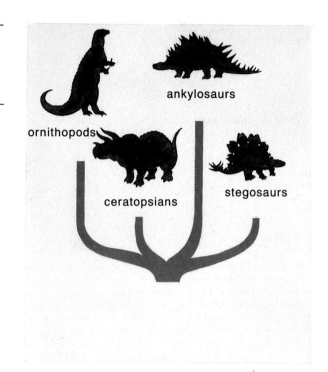

ornithopods

ankylosaurs

ceratopsians

stegosaurs

Our chart shows four other groups of dinosaurs that ate plants.

The Iguanodon in our picture was an **ornithopod**.

It was 25 feet tall and 35 feet long. It ate leaves and twigs. It had strong back legs to run away from its enemies.

Stegosaurus

Triceratops

Stegosaurs had huge bony scales on their backs and **spines** on their tails to protect them from the meat-eating dinosaurs.

Triceratops had horns like a rhinoceros for protection, and a bony neck frill.

These dinosaurs walked on four legs. They were very big and heavy and moved very slowly. They lived on grassland and ate plants.

Flying Dinosaurs

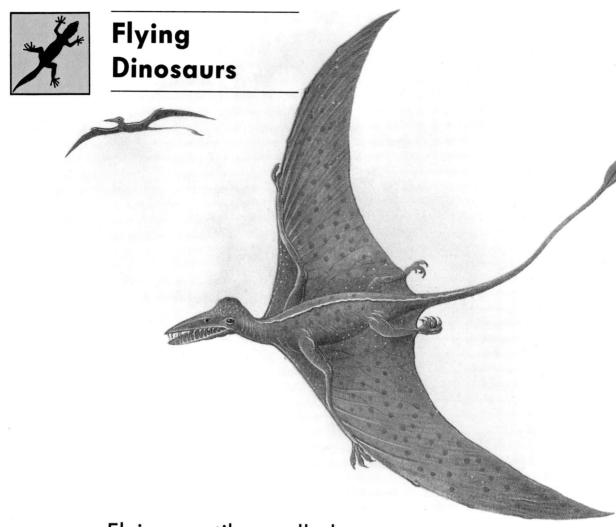

Flying reptiles, called **pterosaurs**, developed from thecodonts.
Most had long mouths and many small teeth.

The Rhamphorynchus in our picture had a long tail and a **wingspan** of three feet. It used its long tail to steer with and change direction in flight.

Pteranodon

The Pteranodon in our picture was the largest flying reptile.

It had a wingspan of over 23 feet. It lived along coasts and glided off the cliffs.

Birds developed from the **Archaeopteryx**, which had feathers like a bird and the body of a reptile.

Archaeopteryx

Sea Reptiles

Most early reptiles lived on dry land. Reptiles called **ichthyosaurs** lived in the sea.

They looked similar to dolphins with long mouths and many tiny teeth.

an ichthyosaur

Mosasaurs also lived in the sea.

They grew over 30 feet long. They had big mouths and long tails.

They hunted and ate other sea creatures.

a mosasaur

The plesiosaurs in our picture were
25 feet long.
   They had long necks and legs shaped
like paddles. They could swim well.
Their big jaws had many teeth. They
hunted and ate fish.

The End of the Dinosaurs

Some scientists think the dinosaurs died out because the **climate** changed and the weather became too hot for them.

The plants and forests dried up so there was no food for the plant-eating dinosaurs, so they died.

Then the meat-eating dinosaurs had no food and many of them died, too.

After the warm period, the climate grew very cold.

The few remaining dinosaurs could not keep warm. They were too cold to move around. Soon all the dinosaurs died out. The age of reptiles was over.

Mammals and birds slowly took over. They had fur and feathers on their bodies to keep them warm.

it was too cold for dinosaurs

23

Reptiles Today

Our chart shows the four main groups of reptiles that are alive today.

Snakes and lizards are the largest group, with 5,800 different kinds.

There are 230 different types of turtles and tortoises.

There are 22 different kinds of crocodiles and alligators.

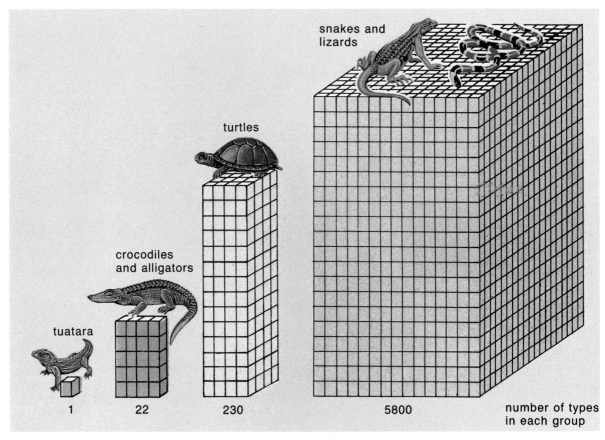

snakes and lizards

turtles

crocodiles and alligators

tuatara

1   22   230   5800   number of types in each group

Our picture shows the tuatara, the
only member of the fourth group.
The tuatara has not changed for
millions of years.

   It lives in **burrows** and comes out at
night to eat insects and spiders.
It grows very slowly and can take 300
years to reach its full size of 24 inches
long.

Where Reptiles Live

Most reptiles live in hot countries, in deserts, or in forests. Reptiles that live in forests live mainly in trees.

Many have strange body shapes or different colors and patterns. They may look like leaves, or stony ground, which helps them hide from their enemies.

The bright colors of the coral snake in our picture warns its enemies to stay away.

Some reptiles on the Galapagos Islands in the Pacific are very large, like the Galapagos turtle. The iguana in our picture also lives on the Galapagos Islands.

Reptiles in the Desert

Reptiles are very good at living in the desert because they do not need to drink much water.

They eat the few insects and the desert plants.

Many dig burrows in the sand.

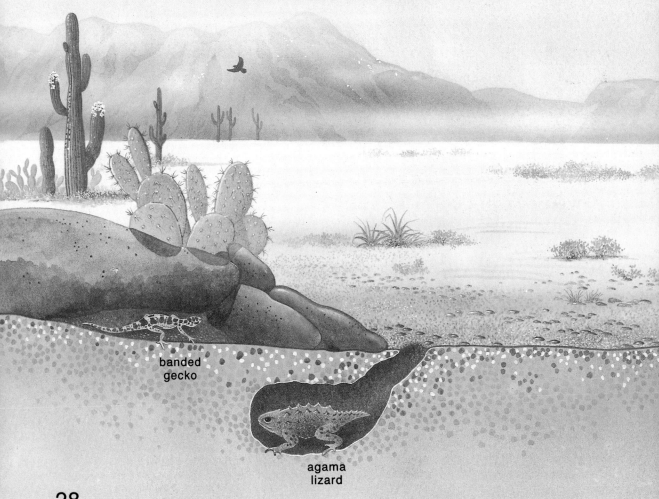

banded
gecko

agama
lizard

The reptiles warm themselves up in the early morning sun.

At midday they find shelter from the hot sun in their burrows, or in the shade of the rocks.

At night the desert can be quite cold, so the reptiles keep warm in their burrows.

They lay their eggs in their burrows. This keeps the eggs warm and helps them to hatch.

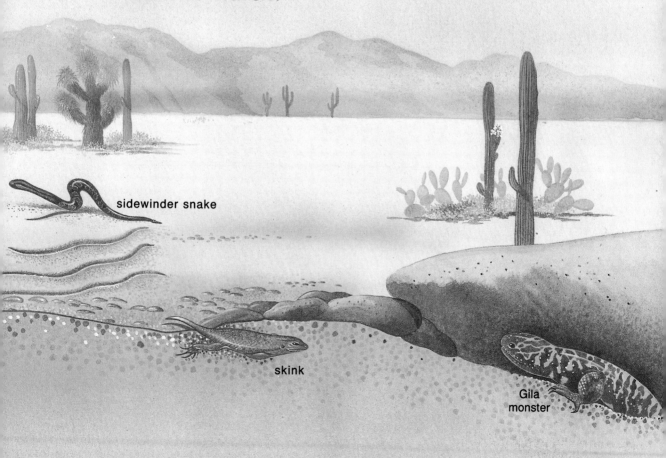

sidewinder snake

skink

Gila monster

Lizards

Lizards are all different shapes, sizes, and colors. The smallest is the gecko lizard, which is only 7.5 inches long. The largest is the Komodo dragon, which grows up to 10 feet long.

a Komodo dragon

some different lizards

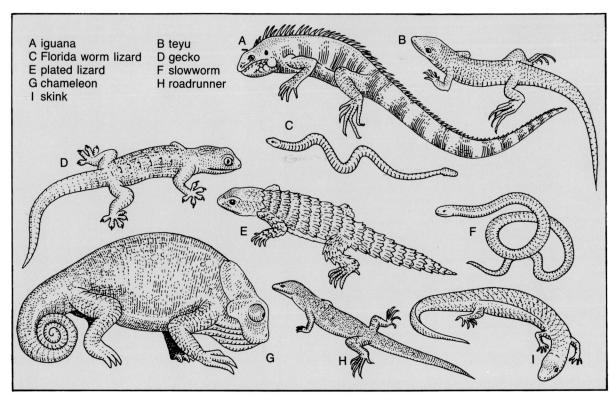

A iguana
C Florida worm lizard
E plated lizard
G chameleon
I skink

B teyu
D gecko
F slowworm
H roadrunner

30

Most lizards live in burrows and eat insects.

The largest lizards live in Africa, Asia, and Australia.

Some lizards live in cool countries. These lizards **hibernate** during the cold winter

The red lines in our picture show how a lizard moves. The whole body wriggles from side to side like a fish. Its long tail helps keep the lizard balanced.

Most lizards can break off their tails and grow new ones, so they can escape if an enemy grabs them by the tail.

Some Strange Lizards

Our picture shows a chameleon. It has a long sticky tongue which flicks out to catch flies.

Chameleons can change color to match the colors around them.

Many lizards are odd shapes.

They have spines or **crests** to protect them from their enemies.

The armadillo lizard in our picture curls up into a prickly ball if it is attacked.

Most animals find this ring of sharp spines is too prickly to eat.

a frilled lizard

The frilled lizard looks very fierce when it is attacked. It raises its large neck frill and hisses loudly.

an armadillo lizard

Snakes

Anacondas are the biggest snakes in the world.

Anacondas and pythons are not poisonous like rattlesnakes, adders, and cobras.

snakes are different sizes

When a viper opens its mouth to strike its **prey**, the poisonous **fangs** flick forward.

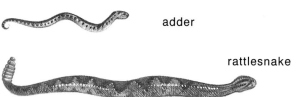

adder

rattlesnake

cobra

python

anaconda

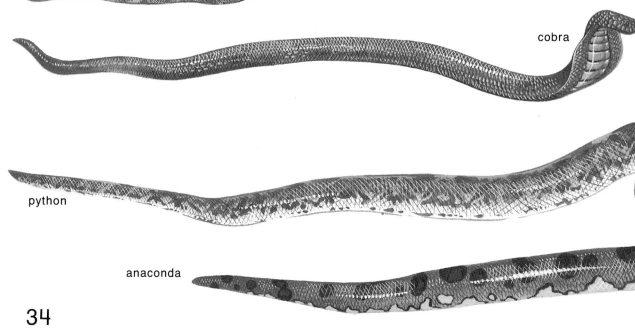

Look how snakes move.
1. This snake coils up, then darts its head forward so the neck pulls the rest of the body along.

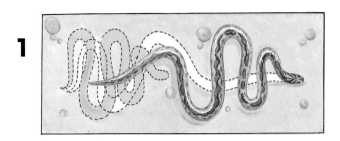

2. This snake moves in curves, pushing against stones and things in its path.

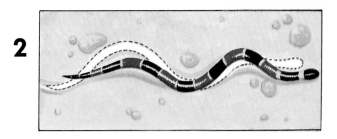

3. This snake rolls its body along in loops, hardly touching the ground.

4. Big snakes grip the ground with their scales and pull themselves forward.

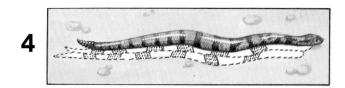

Snakes on the Attack

Snakes eat small animals, birds, insects, lizards, fish, or eggs.

Some snakes are poisonous and kill by injecting **venom** into their prey. These snakes have special teeth or fangs where they store the poison.

Can you see the fangs in the mouth of this rattlesnake?

Other snakes, like the emerald boa in
our picture, use their strong bodies
to kill their prey.

They grab their prey with their
powerful jaws and wrap their bodies
around the animal. Then they squeeze
so tight that the animal cannot breathe.

These snakes are called **constrictors**.

Crocodiles and Alligators

Most crocodiles and alligators are found near fresh water.

A few, like the saltwater crocodile in our picture, live in places where rivers flow into the sea and the water is salty.

These saltwater crocodiles grow up to 20 feet in length. They have long powerful tails and large mouths with many teeth.

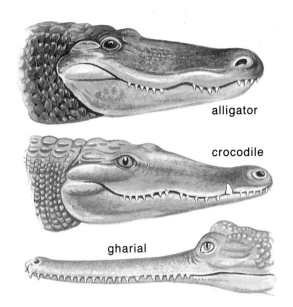

alligator

crocodile

gharial

**look at their teeth
and snouts**

A crocodile has a long lower tooth that shows when it closes its mouth.

Alligators have more rounded snouts than crocodiles.

A gharial is like a crocodile, but it has a long thin snout.

Our picture shows an alligator in a swamp.

Tortoises and Turtles

Giant tortoises are only found on islands in the Pacific and Indian Oceans.

They can live for over 100 years.

The giant tortoise in our picture will grow to be five feet long. It has a hard shell to protect its body.

Giant tortoises eat plants and live on the land. They sit in the sun to keep warm.

an adult green turtle

Turtles live in rivers and the sea.

Green turtles live in the sea for the first ten years of their life. Then they return to the beaches where they were hatched.

The female turtle crawls up the beach. She lays her eggs in a hole in the sand.

When the eggs hatch, the baby turtles crawl back down the beach to the sea.

Enemies

Reptiles have many enemies.
Birds and mammals like to eat them.
    This secretary bird is keeping a
look out for snakes. It kills snakes
with the powerful **talons** on its feet.

Sea birds eat baby turtles as they make their way down to the sea.

Other animals such as rats like eating the eggs of snakes.

The hedgehog is a good hunter. It kills and eats adders.

The spines on its back protect the hedgehog from the snake.

The mongoose in our picture is a good snake hunter, too. It will attack and kill a cobra twice its size.

It seizes the snake behind the head and shakes the snake until it is dead.

The Future

Many people think that all snakes should be killed because they are poisonous.

Many snakes and lizards are harmless. They help us by eating rats and other pests.

Some people kill reptiles for their skins or for food. Other people take their eggs.

Forest fires also kill many reptiles.

Some reptiles like the green turtle are now very rare.

a forest fire

a green turtle

Many reptiles are in danger of becoming **extinct** because people have drained the swamps and cut down the forests where they live.

Our picture shows a Gila monster which is an **endangered** wild animal. Laws now stop people from killing the Gila monster.

a Gila monster

Glossary

amphibian an animal that can live on water or on land. Frogs, toads, newts, and salamanders are amphibians.

ankylosaur a type of dinosaur that ate plants. It had a tough skin that was like heavy armor.

archaeopteryx half reptile, half bird, this animal had feathered wings. It was not a good flyer and probably glided between trees.

burrows holes dug in the ground by animals where they can shelter and lay their eggs.

ceratopsians a group of dinosaurs with bony horns and huge bony neck frills.

climate the weather of an area or country during the year. Deserts have hot dry climates. Mountain tops have cold climates.

constrictors a type of snake that kills its prey by winding its body around the animal and squeezing hard so it stops breathing.

crest raised portion on the head to give protection against enemies.

dinosaur a group of reptiles that lived on Earth long ago. Dinosaurs had legs underneath their bodies.

endangered any kind of animal or plant that is in danger of dying out.

extinct an animal or plant that has died out.

fang a sharp curved tooth. The fangs of snakes may be hollow. Fangs are often used to squirt poison into the prey.

fossils the remains of animals or plants, usually found in rocks. A fossil can be the bones of an animal or the shape left by an animal's body in the rock.

hibernate to ''sleep'' or stay still during the cold winter.

ichthyosaur a type of reptile that lived in the seas when dinosaurs lived on the land.

mammal an animal with a warm body that is usually covered with fur. Mammals give birth to live young which feed on the mother's milk.

mosasaur a group of early reptiles that lived in the sea. Mosasaurs were long fierce reptiles with large teeth.

ornithopod one of a group of dinosaurs that ran on their back legs. The feet of ornithopods looked like birds' feet.

prey an animal that is hunted and eaten by other animals.

pterosaur a type of reptile with wings. Some pterosaurs were the size of small birds, others grew very large. Pterosaurs probably glided through the air.

sauropod a group of dinosaurs that ate plants. They had long tails and necks.

skeleton the hard bony parts of an animal that give the animals its shape.

spines sharp pointed parts on the animal's back to give it protection.

stegosaur a type of plant-eating dinosaur with large bony spines along its back.

swamps low-lying ground where there is a lot of water.

talons sharp, hooked claws of a bird of prey.

thecodont one of a group of meat-eating dinosaurs that lived 225 million years ago. Many types of dinosaur descended from it.

theropod one of a large group of dinosaurs that included all meat-eaters. They probably walked on their hind legs.

venom the poison made by snakes.

wingspan the measurement across both wings, from wing tip to wing tip.

Early reptiles that appear in this book

Euparkeria
Tyrannosaurus
Brachiosaurus
Coelophysis
Diplodocus
Dimetrodon
Iguanodon

Triceratops
Pteranodon
Rhamphorynchus
Seymouria
Archaeopteryx
Plesiosaurus
Ornithomimus

Index

Acknowledgments
The Publishers wish to thank the Australian Information Service, London for their invaluable assistance in the preparation of this book.
Photographic credits (t = top b = bottom l = left r = right)
Cover and title page photographs: Frank Lane Picture Agency; 8b ZEFA; 9 Anthony Bannister/NHPA: 11t ZEFA; 11b P. Green/Ardea London; 25 M.F. Soper/NHPA; 26 James Carmichael/NHPA; 27 ZEFA; 30/31 Philippa Scott/NHPA; 32 Stephen Dalton/NHPA; 33t Douglas Baglin/NHPA: 36 Stephen Dalton/NHPA; 37 James Carmichael/NHPA; 38 L.H. Newman/NHPA; 39 ZEFA; 40 Peter Johnson/NHPA; 41t Bill Wood/NHPA; 42 Aquila; 43 Michael Leach/NHPA; 44b Philippa Scott/NHPA; 44/45 Australian Information Service, London; 45b Stephen Kraseman/NHPA.